FISH RIDDLES

Library of Congress Catalog-in-Publication Data
Woodworth, Viki
Fish riddles / Written and illustrated by Viki Woodworth.
p. cm.
Summary: A collection of riddles relating to fish.
Example: How did the dogfish
pay for dinner? With her credit cod.
ISBN 1-56766-065-7
1. Wit and humor, Juvenile 2. Fishes–Juvenile humor.
[1. Food–Wit and humor   2. Jokes.]
I. Title.
PN6163.W68 1994   92-34646
818.5402–dc20   CIP/AC

FISH RIDDLES

Compiled and Illustrated by
Viki Woodworth

Why doesn't the ocean say goodbye?
It prefers to wave.

What do you call an underwater hot spring?
A fish fry.

What did the rock say to the barnacle?
"Get off my back!"

What did the barnacle say to the rock?
"But I'm stuck on you."

What did one rock say to the other rock?
"Ooh, I love your mussels!"

What do you call a fish who drives underwater?
A scuba driver.

Do fish believe tall tales?
Yes, they swallow them hook, line and sinker.

What do fish lawyers do?
Read gills.

Why couldn't the fish quit his bad habit?
He was hooked.

Why did the fish talk so long on the phone?
It couldn't get off the line.

What language do fish speak?
Finnish.

When does a fish stop eating?
When it's stuffed.

What's another name for confused caviar?
Scrambled eggs.

What's another name for mean caviar?
Deviled eggs.

What's another name for well-taken care of caviar?
Coddled eggs.

What did the sardine say when she opened the can?
"My it's close in here!"

What do you call a sardine that's been kicked out of school?
Canned.

What do sharks eat with baked beans?
Sardini-wienies.

What book do fish love to read?
Huckleberry Fins.

What did the Little Pig build his underwater house out of?
Fish sticks.

Why couldn't the Big Bad Wolf blow down the fish stick house?
He huffed and puffed and swallowed water.

What does Pinnochio become when he's shipwrecked?
Driftwood.

What fish tale is about a beautiful fish princess who travels a lot?
Snow White and the Seven Wharves.

What fish tale is about a poor fish with a wicked stepmother?
Finderella.

Why didn't the swordfish win the first race?
Only his nose was running.

Did the swordfish win the second race?
Yes, by a nose.

Why did the shark eat the boat's anchor rope?
The dentist told him to floss.

What did the fish say to the shark?
I get the point.

What candy does a shark hang on it's Christmas Tree?
Hurri-canes.

Why do sharks do well in business?
They can make snap decisions.

What do you call an octopus who sticks to a rock all day?
An all day sucker.

What does an octopus become when it eats a lemon?
An octosourpus.

What do you call an octopus who loves classical music?
A Bachtopus.

Why didn't the octopus write her book report?
She ran out of ink.

Why don't octopus build snowmen?
They can't find mittens to fit them.

What do you have when an octopus goes hiking?
An Octo Puss 'n Boots.

Why is the ocean hard to get along with?
It likes to make waves.

What makes the ocean grouchy?
Being crossed.

Which sea creature talks the most?
The whale—it's always spouting off.

What fish is worth a lot?
A goldfish.

How can you keep a fish from smelling?
Hold it's nose.

Why doesn't anyone like the crab?
Because he's shellfish.

What fish flies to the moon?
A Lunar tuna.

What do you hear when you tell jokes to a can of tuna?
Canned laughter.

How did the tuna borrow books?
With it's library cod.

What do you get when you break a sand dollar?
Change.

Why did the mermaid throw away the sand dollar?
It was counterfeit.

How can you tell when a mermaid is in love?

She has starfish in her eyes.

What do you call a fish who jumps into a musical instrument?

A tuba diver.

What do you call a musical fish?

A tooney fish.

Which fish sings in the choir?

The bass.

Why didn't they let the mermaid sing in the choir?

She couldn't carry a tuna.

Which fish can really sing loudly?

The whaler.

Who plays the harp in the orchestra?
The angelfish.

21

How did the flounder feel?
A little flat.

When did the flounder feel even worse?
When it hit bottom.

What did the flounder say to the salmon?
How is life at the top?

What do you call a helium filled tiny sea creature?
A shrimp blimp.

What do you call an angry shrimp?
Fried.

How did the boxer shrimp feel after the fight?
Battered.